BRANDON GRAY

Become A Physical Therapist: A Comprehensive Step by Step Guide for Aspiring Physical Therapists

ISBN 979-8-9884581-0-4 (Paperback)

ISBN 979-8-9884581-1-1 (Ebook)

ISBN 979-8-9884581-2-8 (Hardcover)

First edition

Cover art by MiBlart

This book was professionally typeset on Reedsy.
Find out more at reedsy.com

This book is dedicated to all those who became what they didn't see and made it possible for others to become.

"You must know where you want to go before you can plan a route to get there."

-Brandon Gray

Contents

Preface   ii

Chapter 1   1

  WHO ARE PHYSICAL THERAPISTS?   1

Chapter 2   5

  A BRIEF HISTORY OF THE PHYSICAL THERAPY PROFES-
SION IN THE UNITED STATES   5

Chapter 3   10

  CHOOSE YOUR MAJOR IN UNDERGRAD   10

Chapter 4   13

  GET INTO PHYSICAL THERAPY SCHOOL   13

Chapter 5   26

  TIPS FOR SHADOWING/OBSERVING A PHYSICAL THERAPIST   26

Chapter 6   28

  COMMON INTERVIEW QUESTIONS AND HOW TO ANSWER   28

Chapter 7   33

  SET YOURSELF APART   33

Chapter 8   38

  CHOOSE THE RIGHT PHYSICAL THERAPY SCHOOL   38

Chapter 9   42

  SURVIVING PHYSICAL THERAPY SCHOOL   42

Chapter 10   47

  PREPARING FOR THE BOARDS   47

REFERENCES   52

APPENDIX   54

ABOUT THE AUTHOR   57

Conclusion   58

Preface

Sometimes being book smart isn't enough to get you to where you want to go. Sometimes becoming what you want to become is not a straight and well defined path. Becoming a physical therapist should not be one of these times. However, for many people aspiring to become a physical therapist who are trying to navigate the winding and very competitive road, there is sometimes no road map or any clearly defined directions. This was the case for me and the reason for this book.

According to the American Physical Therapy Association, The average acceptance rate for physical therapy schools in the U.S.was approximately 59% for the 2017-2018 and 2018-2019 academic years. With an extremely competitive process and the amount of misinformation about the physical therapy profession, the process to become a physical therapist will require more than passing a test and a good G.P.A. It will require deliberate planning to ensure that you are on the right road.

The purpose of this book is to provide you with a clear path with the steps you should follow to get into physical therapy school and provide tips and tools that you will need to help you ultimately become a physical therapist. This book provides information on all three phases of becoming a physical therapist: getting into physical therapy school, what to do while in physical therapy school to ensure you graduate, and tips on how to pass the boards after you graduate. Whether you are a high school student who is considering physical therapy as a career, a college student who is graduating with your bachelors degree and getting ready to apply to physical therapy school, or a professional looking for a second career, this book will provide you with the information and tips to place you on the correct path to become a physical therapist.

Chapter 1

WHO ARE PHYSICAL THERAPISTS?

The confusion about the identity of who physical therapists are continues to be an issue in the general public. Some people think physical therapists are the same as athletic trainers, massage therapists, or chiropractors. Others believe physical therapists only help people who are injured walk again. Many people do not know the educational requirements it takes to become a physical therapist or that physical therapists must have a doctoral level degree. As a future physical therapist, it is important to have a thorough understanding of the profession and to be able to educate and communicate to the public about who physical therapists are and the benefits of physical therapy treatment.

Physical therapists are doctoral level educated, licensed clinicians who diagnose and treat individuals of all ages who have injuries, disabilities, and other health conditions that affect movement and quality of life. They also develop programs to reduce injury risk (injury prevention) and help people who want to improve their overall health (wellness). The American Physical Therapy Association (APTA) defines physical therapists with a simpler definition:

Physical therapists are educated, licensed clinicians and movement experts who improve quality of life through hands-on care, patient education, and prescribed movement.

Physical therapists perform examinations, review the findings of the examinations, make a physical therapy diagnosis (functional diagnosis), then develop treatment plans to improve one's ability to perform normal movement, manage pain, restore normal function, reduce risk of re-injury, and reduce risk of disability.

From simple sprains and strains to surgeries to significant developmental disabilities, physical therapists work with a variety of patient populations with movement-related issues.

Where Do Physical Therapists Work?

Physical Therapists work in a variety of different settings. A therapist's role will vary based on the type of patient and condition being treated or the job being performed. Some of the common settings and areas include:

- Hospitals
    - Rehabilitation Hospitals/ Centers
    - Skilled Nursing Facilities (SNF)
    - Long Term Acute Care Facilities (LTAC)
    - Outpatient Clinics
    - Private Practice
    - Home Health
    - Schools
    - Sports Organizations
    - Industrial Facilities
    - University (Education and Research)
    - Consulting
    - Telehealth
    - Concierge

Education:

Physical therapists in the United States (US) must earn a doctor of physical therapy degree from a program accredited by the Commission on the Accreditation in Physical Therapy Education (CAPTE). As of December 2020, there were 262 programs accredited by CAPTE and fifty-seven developing programs. The average length of a physical therapy program is three years.

Licensure:

To practice as a physical therapist in the US, graduates from accredited physical therapy programs must take and pass the National Physical Therapy Examination (NPTE). Graduates from both United States programs and international programs must take the NPTE. The NPTE is administered by the Federation of State Boards of Physical Therapy (FSBPT). The exam is offered once each quarter in January, April, July, and October.

Specialization:

The APTA established the physical therapy specialization program in 1978. Currently there are ten areas in which physical therapists can gain specialty certification. The areas of specialty are:

- Cardiovascular & Pulmonary
- Clinical Electrophysiology
- Oncology
- Women's Health
- Wound Management
- Geriatrics
- Neurology
- Orthopedics
- Pediatrics
- Sports

The minimum requirements to become a board-certified specialist include being a currently licensed physical therapist and having a minimum of 2,000 hours of clinical practice in the area in which specialization is being sought. Other requirements vary based on the specific certification area. Physical therapists are trained to treat all patient populations. Specialty certification in the physical therapy profession is optional, physical therapists are not required to hold a specialty certification to practice.

Salary:

Salary is an important consideration when choosing a career. There are many factors that affect physical therapists' salary including area of practice, type and size of company, ownership vs employee, insurance reimbursement rates, etc. While salaries vary, I will include recent salary and job growth figures from the United States Bureau of Labor Statistics (BLS). The BLS predicts a 17% increase in job growth for physical therapists between 2021 and 2031. Physical therapists could expect to earn a median salary of $95,620 with the bottom 10% earning less than $61,930 and the top 10% earning more than $127,110 according to BLS May 2021 reports. Salaries for practice areas during the same period were as follows:

- Home healthcare services: $99,800
- Nursing and residential care facilities: $99,460
- Hospitals (local, state, and private): $99,040
- Private practices (outpatient clinics): $79,470

I encourage you to research current salary data at the time you plan to apply for physical therapy school.

Chapter 2

A BRIEF HISTORY OF THE PHYSICAL THERAPY PROFESSION IN THE UNITED STATES

The foundational principles of physical therapy are documented as early as 3000 B.C. with evidence of Chinese practitioners using massage and exercise to treat injuries. In 430 B.C. Hippocrates is documented to have used massage, manual manipulation, and water therapy for pain relief. However, the origin of physical therapy as an autonomous profession dates back to the early seventeenth century to Pehr Henrik Ling known as the "Father of Swedish Gymnastics" who founded the Royal Central Institute of Gymnastics (RCIG) for exercise, massage, and manipulation. Dr. Ling studied martial arts and a traditional Chinese medicine treatment technique called tui na (pronounced "twee naw") and later divided these into four treatment areas consisting of, medical (physical therapy), military (fencing), pedagogical (physical education), and aesthetics. These principles would be used to treat patients and the RCIG would become the first formally state-sanctioned education program, educating the first physical therapists. Upon completion of the program and passing an examination, the graduates would be given the title, "Director of Gymnastics" (Moffat, 2012).

The term "physiotherapie" would first appear in a published article in 1851 by German military physician, Dr. Lorenz Gleich. Dr. Gleich was a proponent of natural medicine methods that used physical agents such as air, water, light, movement, heat, cold, and electricity to stimulate the body's natural healing powers. The term would later appear again in 1894 as "physiotherapy" in an article in the Montreal Medical Journal by Canadian physician Dr. Edward Playter. The term physiotherapy later evolved into "physical therapy" (Moffat, 2012).

The beginning of physical therapy as a profession in the United States (US) was born from two major historical incidents. 1) Caring for victims of the poliomyelitis (polio) epidemics in the late 1890s who needed rehabilitation due to the effects of the disease. 2) Caring for soldiers who were injured and required rehabilitation during World War I. Dr. Frank Granger, MD (Chief of Orthopedics at Massachusetts General Hospital) and Dr. Joel Goldthwait, MD (Chairman of the War Reconstruction Committee of the American Orthopedic Association), established two groups of medical professionals called "recon-struction aides" to care for wounded soldiers during the first World War. These two groups were physical therapists and occupational therapists. Physical therapists were responsible for providing exercise programs, hydrotherapy, massage, and other modalities for injured soldiers. Early physical therapists would work under physicians, primarily orthopedic physicians, and physical therapy physicians (who would later become known as physiatrists). The first training program was established at Walter Reed General Hospital by Marguerite Sanderson. Mary McMillian, who worked with Marguerite Sanderson at Walter Reed, would later start a program to train reconstruction aides at Reed College in Portland Oregon in 1914 and helped form thirteen additional education programs. According to a Reed College brochure, the 1918 Reconstruction Aide program was a six-week summer program. It accepted women only. The program also required that you were between 25 and 40 years old, 5'0" and 5'8" in height, 100 and 195 pounds in weight. There was rigorous coursework including Anatomy, Physiology, Personal Hygiene, Psychological Aspect of Recovery, Posture, Theory of Bandaging, Military Hospital Management, Practices in Massage, Corrective Gymnastics and Other Remedial Exercises, Clinics in Orthopedic Surgery, and other courses. The women were also required to take part in daily physical fitness activities. The cost of the program was fifty dollars (Moffat, 2003, 2012; Vogel 1967).

As the profession continued to grow, it became universally understood that the need for a professional organization was essential. At that time, the profession was made up of women. Subsequently, the American Women's Physiotherapeutic Association (AWPA) was formed in 1921 with Mary McMillan, known as the Mother of Physical Therapy, chosen as the first president. Men began to enter the profession in 1922 and the organization was renamed the American Physiotherapy Association (APA). Physiotherapists would continue to work under the direction of medical doctors and, along with physicians, were members in the American Congress of Rehabilitation Medicine (ACRM) that was formed in 1923. The ACRM included physiotherapists, radiologists, and physical therapy physicians. In 1927 under the APA's second president, Gertrude Beard, the profession's scientific journal, P.T. Review was renamed Physiotherapy Review and there was an increased focus on improving evidence-based research and implementing evidence-based treatment techniques in clinical practice. The APA changed its name to American Physical Therapy Association (APTA) in 1946 after physicians specializing in rehabilitation (physical therapy physicians) changed their professional title to "physiatrist." Simultaneously, the passage of the Hospital Survey and Construction Act of 1946 (The Hill-Burton Act) which mandated the construction of new hospitals across the country led to an increase in hospital-based physical therapy practice. (Moffat, 2003)

Physical therapy education programs were certificate-based programs until 1927 when the first bachelor's degree program was established at New York University (NYU). As the field continued to grow, it was understood that there was a need for practicing therapists to maintain and advance their clinical skills. The response came in 1941 when the first continuing education courses began to be offered during the APA's annual conference. NYU later established the first master's degree program in 1942. The profession would also later respond to the need of a lack of diversity with the formation of The

Special Women's Medical Service Corps for African-American Women. This organization, launched in 1943, would help fulfill the need for physical therapy services for African-American soldiers. One of the most famous women of this early group of black physical therapists was Bessie Virginia Blount who was known for inventing a feeding device to assist injured soldiers with eating. The device was made up of a tube that delivered individual pieces of food at the patient's pace. She later modified the device and received a patent. (Moffat, 2003).

Physical therapy continued to transition from hospital-based programs to university-based academic programs from the late 1950s to the late 1970s. The bachelor's degree became the required degree to enter the profession in 1978. The first post-professional transitional doctor of physical therapy (t-DPT) program was established in 1992 at the University of Southern California (USC). Creighton University created the first entry- level doctor of physical therapy (DPT) program in 1993. In 2004, the Commission on Accreditation of Physical Therapy Education (CAPTE) stated that the DPT was the preferred degree to enter the physical therapy profession and in 2015 the DPT became the only degree awarded by accredited programs. (Moffat, 2003, 2012).

The physical therapy profession also gained more autonomy as physical therapists transitioned from technicians to professional practitioners from the 1950s thru the 1970s during the Korean War and the Vietnam War. One event that aided this transition was the formation of the Self-Employed section of the APTA and the development of a standardized seven-hour professional competency exam. The exam was called the APTA- PES Exam (APTA-Professional Examination Service). It consisted of 310 questions and covered topics including basic sciences, clinical sciences, and theory and procedures. The field of cardiopulmonary rehabilitation also recognized a need for more physical therapists as doctors began to accept research that showed prolonged bedrest and inactivity after myocardial infarctions increased complications. During the late sixties to late seventies there was an expansion of physical therapy into orthopedics due to an increase in joint replacement surgeries (Moffat, 2003).

In the twenty-first century, physical therapists are growing into completely autonomous clinicians who can evaluate and treat individuals with various neuromusculoskeletal disorders and movement dysfunction without a physician's referral. As of 2017 all fifty US states as well as the US Virgin Islands and Washington, DC have some form of direct access that allows patients to receive treatment from a physical therapist without a physician referral. The profession is continuing to grow as physical therapists advance the profession by moving outside the walls of traditional hospital-based practices and practices owned by large corporations into private practices, physical therapists-owned companies, concierge practices, and virtual practices. It is essential to the profession's longevity for new therapists to continue advancing treatment methods with evidence-based practice and advocating for legislation to protect the profession.

Chapter 3

CHOOSE YOUR MAJOR IN UNDERGRAD

When you enter college, choosing a major can be stressful. Selecting the right major can be even more challenging when your goal is to become a physical therapist. In this chapter, we will simplify the process of choosing a major and provide you with tips about the most common majors for students entering physical therapy school.

There is no specific degree requirement to enter physical therapy school. You may get your undergraduate degree in whatever area you choose. However, the most important thing to remember when deciding which major to choose is to verify that the courses taken in undergrad satisfy the prerequisites of the physical therapy programs to which you plan to apply. Although the specific prerequisites for physical therapy schools vary, most science-based majors such as biology or kinesiology will meet all or most of the prerequisites for physical therapy programs. If you want to choose a non-science degree such as English, you will need to make sure that the required prerequisite courses are completed. As part of the degree program, you will need to take "elective" courses. Elective courses are extra classes that count toward the hours needed for a degree, but these classes may not be directly related to your degree program. If you choose a major that does not satisfy all the necessary prerequisites, you will need to take the required courses as elective classes.

An example of this would be, you are an English major but chemistry I and II are required to get into physical therapy school. Chemistry I and II are not usually taken as part of the English degree curriculum but can be taken as electives courses. Therefore, taking chemistry I and II as electives will allow the requirement to be met.

Physical Therapy Centralized Application Service (PTCAS) identifies the following courses as the most common prerequisites for physical therapy programs (Be aware that each physical therapy program may require different prerequisite courses.):

- Anatomy and Physiology I & II
- Biology I & II
- Chemistry I & II
- Physics I & II
- Psychology
- Statistics
- Exercise Physiology
- Medical Terminology
- English
- Communications
- Humanities
- Ethics
- First Aid/CPR
- Nutrition, Health/Wellness
- Math (e.g., college algebra)

While you may obtain your bachelor's degree in whatever area you choose, admission statistics show there are common majors among applicants who are admitted into physical therapy school. Here are the top ten majors for applicants accepted into physical therapy school according to PTCAS:

1. Exercise Science
2. Kinesiology
3. Biology
4. Health Sciences
5. Psychology
6. Athletic Training
7. Pre-physical Therapy
8. General Studies
9. Biological Sciences
10. Physiology

(Source: Physical Therapy Centralized Application Service,2019)

With an understanding of the required prerequisites and the most common majors for acceptance into physical therapy programs, you can now work with your academic advisor or guidance counselor to help you choose the academic track that allows you to graduate with the degree you want while satisfying the requirements for a competitive physical therapy school application.

Chapter 4

GET INTO PHYSICAL THERAPY SCHOOL

The application process for most programs is administered by the Physical Therapy Centralized Application Service (PTCAS). Admission into a doctor of physical therapy program in the US will require some or all of the following:

- Bachelor's degree: a bachelor's degree with completion of specific prerequisite courses (see Chapter 3 for a list of prerequisite courses)
- GRE: a GRE score above the 50th percentile in each of the three sections. The three sections are verbal, quantitative, and analytical.
- Observation Hours: Physical Therapy programs that require observation hours, require between 20 and 100 hours depending on the program. Some programs "recommend" up to 300 hours. (I place quotation marks here because any recommendation made by the program should be taken as a requirement. If the university recommends 300 hours, you should get 300 hours)
- Undergraduate GPA: above 3.50
- Completion of a personal statement or essay
- Letters of recommendation: (The number of letters required will vary by program)
- Interview

Acceptance into a physical therapy program is an extremely competitive process. Remember that you are competing with other students who are just as smart and just as accomplished as you. Based on data from PTCAS (American Physical Therapy Association 2020), the average GPA for candidates accepted into physical therapy programs in 2019 was 3.58, while the average GPA for all applicants was 3.43. The average GRE Scores for accepted applicants in 2018-2019 were 61.61% for the verbal section, 51.74% for the quantitative section, and 52.66% for the analytical section. In the 2018-2019 reporting period a total of 17,834 individuals applied to physical therapy schools, and 10,578 students were accepted. The top majors for physical therapy applicants were exercise science, kinesiology, biology, health science, and psychology.

PTCAS Applicants by Race and Ethnicity Designations

Race/Ethnicity Designations	Total Applicants in PTCAS		Total Accepted Applicants in PTCAS	
	#	%	#	%
American Indian	177	0.89%	82	0.70%
Asian	2,382	11.91%	1,351	11.49%
Black or African American	1,463	7.32%	573	4.87%
Pacific Islander / Hawaiian	101	0.51%	59	0.50%
Hispanic	2,057	10.29%	1,000	8.50%
White	13,447	67.24%	8,471	72.03%
Did Not Report	373	1.87%	225	1.91%
Total	20,000	100%	11,761	100%

(Reprinted from Physical Therapy Centralized Application Service 2018–2019 Applicant Data Report, with permission of the American Physical Therapy Association. © 2020 American Physical Therapy Association. All Rights Reserved)

Obtaining a high GPA and test scores in the upper percentile alone will not get you into physical therapy school. You must also make it through the application process and the interview. Once you have made the decision that you want to become a physical therapist, it is essential to design a plan to ensure that you are the most competitive applicant that you can be. Do not strive to only meet the basic requirements to get into physical therapy school, you want to try to exceed those requirements. If you do not know what the requirements are or where to start, don't worry, the steps below will help provide you with the most common requirements for physical therapy school.

Step 1: Shadow a Physical Therapist/ Observation Hours

To gain an understanding of how physical therapists work, it's important to shadow many different therapists in as many different settings as possible. This will allow you to gain a greater understanding of the profession, learn how therapists collaborate with other physical therapists and other healthcare professionals, and learn the type of lifestyle a physical therapist lives. Shadowing will also give you the opportunity to learn and ask questions about the physical therapy profession firsthand. Although obtaining observation hours is required by most physical therapy programs, do not think of this as just something you're doing to check a box. Shadowing is for you, not the program you're applying to. You will want to use this time to learn about the different types of patients that physical therapists treat, and the various treatment methods used by physical therapists, as well as ask important questions about salary, lifestyle, work/life balance, or anything that is important to you. Use this time to analyze the profession and determine if it is the right career path for you.

The Commission on Accreditation for Physical Therapy Education (CAPTE) indicates that most physical therapy programs will require anywhere between 50 and 200 observation hours. However, I would recommend prospective students obtain 300-400 hours to provide you with a broader view of the profession and help make you more competitive. Keep in mind that physical therapists work in a variety of different settings. I recommend that you get observation hours in as many different settings as possible. (i.e., outpatient clinics, private practice, hospitals, rehab hospitals, skilled nursing facilities, sports/training gyms, home health/ in-home therapy, industrial facilities). Shadowing in multiple settings allows you to gain a broader understanding of the different patient populations that physical therapists work with and how treatment protocols and techniques differ between those patient groups.

After you decide which facility or clinic you plan to go to for observation hours, contact the facility, let them know you are an aspiring physical therapist, and ask if you may shadow one of the physical therapists at that facility. Document the name of the facility, setting or specialty, therapist name, and number of hours spent shadowing. This documentation will be important once you begin applying to physical therapy programs.

Step 2. Earn a Bachelor's Degree

After graduating from high school, you will need to obtain an undergraduate (bachelors) degree. One of the most important things you will need to decide that will have an impact on your ability to get into physical therapy school is the major you choose while completing your undergraduate studies. As discussed in Chapter 3, when choosing your major, you want to make sure that you choose a major that will satisfy the prerequisite courses that it takes to get into physical therapy school. If you choose a major that does not include the prerequisites, you will need to take the courses that you are missing before applying to physical therapy school. This can have a significant financial impact and increase your overall amount of debt since you will need to pay for these additional courses. To avoid this, I recommend you choose a major that includes the prerequisite courses. Reference the university's course catalog to find the required courses for a major. Most universities have the course catalog posted on their websites. If the course catalog is not posted on the website, contact the university directly and request it.

All accredited physical therapy programs in the US receive accreditation from CAPTE. The prerequisites for each physical therapy program are listed on the CAPTE website. While some of the prerequisites may vary, most physical therapy programs will have similar prerequisite requirements. Most universities now offer a pre-physical therapy track or pre-physical therapy degrees. The pre-physical therapy degree typically satisfies the prerequisites you need to get into physical therapy programs in the US.

If it has been a while since you have been in school or if physical therapy is your second career (or third), it is likely that you will need to complete some of the prerequisite courses to get into a program (see Chapter 3: How to Choose Your Major).

Step 3: Take the GRE

The next thing you will need to do is take the Graduate Record Exam (GRE). The GRE is a standardized exam developed by Educational Testing Service (www.ETS.org). You may be thinking, "Not another standardized test." But the GRE was established in 1936 so it probably is not going anywhere anytime soon. There are a few physical therapy programs that do not require the GRE, but it is required for the majority of physical therapy programs in the US. This will likely be a requirement for the program you will be applying to.

The GRE measures verbal reasoning, quantitative reasoning, critical thinking, and analytical writing skills. It is scored in three test sections: analytical writing, verbal reasoning, and quantitative reasoning. The total exam time is approximately three hours and forty-five minutes. There are a total of six sections with a one-minute break between sections and a ten-minute break after the third section. The analytical writing section has two thirty-minute tasks. One task will require you to analyze an issue and the other will require you to analyze an argument. The verbal reasoning and quantitative reasoning sections are each divided into two twenty-question sections with thirty minutes per section and thirty-five minutes per section respectively. A research section and an unscored section may also be included. The research and unscored sections do not count toward the total score.

The GRE is scored on a scale from 130 to 170. If you're familiar with the GRE, you will know the scoring scale was revised. Prior to the revision of the test, the scoring scale was 200-800. PTCAS reports show most physical therapy students score above the 60th percentile. The average GRE percentile scores for accepted applicants in 2018-2019 were 61.61% for the verbal section, 51.74% for the quantitative section, and 52.66% for the analytical section.

There are several GRE study guides and prep courses to help you prepare for the exam. Many undergraduate colleges/ universities also offer courses to help you prepare for the exam.

Step 4: Apply to Physical Therapy School

The next step is to apply to a physical therapy school. First, before applying to any physical therapy program, review the program's requirements and make sure you meet all of them before applying. I do not recommend you apply to programs if you do not meet all the requirements, as you may waste a lot of time and money. When applying to physical therapy programs you want to apply to as many programs as possible. This will increase your chances of getting accepted into one of the programs. The physical therapy application process is overseen by the Physical Therapy Centralized Application Service (PTCAS). The PTCAS application process will allow you to apply to multiple schools at the same time. The application fee for the most recent application period was $155 for the first program and $60 for each additional program. The application process may require letters of recommendation and a personal statement or essay.

When applying to physical therapy school through the PTCAS process read and follow all instructions on the PTCAS website. Pay close attention to the application deadlines. There are two types of deadlines when applying to physical therapy school, firm deadlines, and soft deadlines. Firm deadlines are deadlines in which applications are due on the specified date and cannot be submitted after the due date. Soft deadlines are deadlines that allow applications to be submitted after the deadline. However, it is important to know that applications received after the due date will receive lower priority or may not be considered at all. In either case, whether your prospective program has a firm or soft deadline, do not miss the deadline. You should try to submit your application as early as possible before the due date.

Step 5: Letters of Recommendation

Many, if not all, physical therapy programs require one or more letters of recommendation as part of the application process. By definition, a letter of recommendation is a formal document that validates a person's work, skills, or academic performance. Your letter of recommendation for physical therapy school should highlight those attributes, but should also focus on strong personality traits, leadership qualities, leadership positions held, and extracurricular activities.

Before you ask someone for a letter of recommendation, consider the following questions:

- How well does the person know you?

- Does the person know your goals?

- Does the person know your academic and extracurricular accomplishments?

- Does the person know your personal attributes that would make you a good physical therapist?

You may be wondering, "Who should I ask?" Your letters should come from a combination of established professionals. You want to try to get letters from physical therapists, professors, supervisors, or managers. Your letters of recommendation should come from people who know you well and can attest to your academic qualities, work ethic, personality traits, and leadership skills. It is not recommended that you get letters from friends or family, because letters from friends and family are usually biased and not as objective compared to letters from professionals. You should have established relationships with the people you ask to write your recommendations. Also, let the writer know exactly what you need. Provide them with your resume/curriculum vitae and a list of your awards and accomplishments. This will allow them to write a recommendation letter that gives the admission staff a multi-dimensional picture of who you are.

When requesting letters of recommendation, consider the person's time you're requesting the letter from. Do not wait until the last minute to complete your application and request a letter of recommendation. The professional you are asking may have professional or family obligations prohibiting them from immediately writing a letter of recommendation. Give them time. I recommend requesting letters a minimum of four weeks before the due date.

Step 6: Personal Statement/ Essay

You are more than your GPA. This is the purpose of your personal statement or essay. The physical therapy programs that you are applying to need to know who you are beyond the numerical evaluation of your academic achievement. A personal statement is your opportunity to highlight your personality, background, and interests. Some personal statements are part of the application and are submitted with your application packet. In addition to a personal statement that may be required by the school, the PTCAS will also include an essay prompt. This prompt changes regularly. When answering the PTCAS essay prompt, thoroughly read the question, understand what is being asked, and reply accordingly.

When writing your personal statement, remember to be authentic, be yourself, and make it personal. Try to avoid giving general answers such as "I want to be a physical therapist because I like helping people." This is too general of an answer since most healthcare professionals like to help people. Try to be specific and personal. Allow the admissions staff to get to know your personal reasons for wanting to become a physical therapist and why you are passionate about it.

If an essay is required, it is likely you will not know the topic until your interview or during the application process. Make sure your essay is concise, structured, and on topic. A wordy essay just to fill the page is not beneficial in this situation.

Some essays are "on the spot" and part of your interview process. On-the-spot essays allow the admissions team to evaluate your critical thinking skills and quick decision-making skills. Some physical therapy programs may require both a personal statement as part of the application process and an essay as part of the interview process.

To help give you an idea of the type of questions that may be asked as part of the application process, the following are examples of previous PTCAS essay prompts:

Example of past PTCAS personal statement prompts:

1. "Every person has a story that has led them to a career. Since there are a variety of health professions that help others, please go beyond your initial interaction or experience with physical therapy and share the deeper story that has confirmed your decision to specifically pursue physical therapy as your career."

1. "Describe your decision-making process in choosing physical therapy as a career choice versus other health care careers."

Step 7: The Interview

The interview is an especially critical part of the application process. It allows you to show the admissions staff, who you are, beyond your application, essay, and transcripts. A good interview should feel like a comfortable conversation. Think of it as a meeting instead of an interview. Remember, this process is a two-way street. You want to learn as much as you can about what the program can offer you and they want to know what you can offer their program. Try not to be scripted. The admissions staff does not want to hear rehearsed answers to standard questions. Generic or vague answers will not help you stand out. Instead, try to be honest, be genuine, and be yourself. Take the time to learn in-depth about the physical therapy profession before your interview. This includes learning about the different patient populations that physical therapists serve, the history of the profession (see Chapter 2), and state and federal legislative policies that affect physical therapists. It is also important to learn about the university and program you are applying to.

If you are not comfortable with being interviewed, it is recommended that you perform mock interviews. Even if you are a strong interviewer, I still recommend practicing mock interviews. Interviewing is a skill. Just like any other skill, it can be improved with repetition. You should practice both one-on-one and group interviews to be prepared for whichever type of interview the physical therapy program that you are applying to will conduct.

Step 8: Graduate from Physical Therapy School

Acceptance into physical therapy school is a great accomplishment. Graduating from physical therapy school is an even greater accomplishment and gets you one step closer to your ultimate goal of becoming a physical therapist. Most physical therapy programs are three years in length. This is important from both an academic perspective and a financial perspective. The physical therapy curriculum is challenging, and it will require you to have good study skills as well as excellent time management skills. The financial burden of physical therapy school is real. Poor financial planning can lead to more stress.

Without financial distractions and stressors, you improve your ability to focus on the rigorous academic load of the physical therapy program. Whether you will take out student loans, pay out of pocket, or have been awarded a scholarship, you will need a financial plan.

I recommend you consult a financial planner as soon as possible. It is a good idea to interview several financial planners until you find the person who aligns with your long-term financial goals and will be the right fit for you and your money.

Once you graduate from physical therapy school with your doctor of physical therapy degree, the journey is not yet over. You still need to become a physical therapist.

Step 9: Take (and pass) the National Physical Therapy Licensure Exam

To become a licensed physical therapist, you must take the national licensure exam (i.e., board exam). Most states will require background checks in addition to passing the NPTE. Some states will also require you to take an additional jurisprudence exam. A jurisprudence exam covers the laws that apply to the practice of physical therapy. If you plan to relocate, make sure the state you are moving to recognizes the license from your home state. If not, you may have to apply for licensure in that state. Some states will recognize other states' licenses through the Physical Therapy Compact (PT Compact). Information about licensure can be found on your state's physical therapy regulatory board's website. You will also be able to find information about licensure and the PT Compact on the American Physical Therapy Association's (APTA) website.

Step 10: Complete Required Continuing Education

Once you are a licensed physical therapist you can begin your career, however there is one more thing. The learning process is not over. Physical therapists are required to renew their license and complete continuing education activities regularly. There are several types of continuing education courses. Courses are structured as in-person seminars, hands-on labs, or on-line courses. The number of hours needed will vary by state based on its' renewal requirements. Typically, these requirements can be found on the state's physical therapy regulatory agency's website.

Step 11: Residency and Board Specialization (Optional)

As a licensed physical therapist, you may advance your knowledge and skills by completing a board-approved residency or become board-certified in one of the ten specialty areas offered by the APTA American Board of Physical Therapy Specialties (ABPTS).

The American Board of Physical Therapy Residency and Fellowship Education (ABPTRFE) is the governing agency for accreditation for physical therapy residency and fellowship education programs. As of October 2021, there were 347 accredited residency programs and 46 accredited fellowship programs in the US.

The ABPTS is the governing body for the APTA Specialist Certification Program. There are ten areas of specialization in which licensed physical therapists can become certified. Specialist certification is optional and currently not a requirement. The areas of specialization are as follows:

- Cardiovascular & Pulmonary
- Clinical Electrophysiology
- Geriatrics
- Neurology
- Oncology
- Orthopedics
- Pediatrics
- Sports
- Women's Health
- Wound Management

Chapter 5

TIPS FOR SHADOWING/OBSERVING A PHYSICAL THERAPIST

Remember, your shadowing experience is an opportunity for you to learn as much as possible about the profession of physical therapy and the healthcare industry. Do not take this opportunity for granted. Shadowing is a privilege. The facility and therapist that has allowed you to shadow are investing time and resources to ensure that you have a rewarding educational experience. Take advantage of this time.

Here are a few tips to help you make the most of your time:

1. Dress professionally for the environment: If you are unsure of what to wear, ask the staff or the therapist.
2. Wear comfortable shoes: You will do a lot of standing and walking.
3. Arrive on time.
4. Turn your phone off: Pay attention to the therapist whom you are shadowing.
5. Ask questions: Be engaged.
6. Take notes: Create a journal of your experience.
7. Thank the therapist and staff: Send a thank you card or email. Acknowledge the clinic/facility on their social media accounts.

Sample questions to ask when shadowing:

1. Would you do it all again? Why or why not?
2. How much can physical therapists make?
3. Are you happy with your work/ life balance?
4. Did you take out student loans? How long did it take to pay off your loans?
5. What was your experience like in physical therapy school?
6. How does state and federal legislation affect physical therapy?
7. Are there any current state or federal bills being considered that will affect physical therapists?
8. How does insurance reimbursement work?
9. How do you choose which continuing education courses to take?
10. How did you choose which setting to work in? (outpatient, inpatient, rehabilitation hospital, skilled nursing facility, home health, etc.)

Chapter 6

COMMON INTERVIEW QUESTIONS AND HOW TO ANSWER

As we discussed in chapter 4, think of the interview as a conversation. To better understand this concept, let's look at the definition of these two words as defined by Merriam-Webster:

Interview- noun: A formal consultation usually to evaluate qualifications (as of a prospective student or employee)

Conversation- noun: the oral exchange of sentiments, observations, or opinions, or ideas. An informal talk involving two people or a small group of people.

When you view the interview as an informal exchange of observations and ideas instead of a formal evaluation of your qualifications, it reduces anxiety and allows you to be more engaged, more interactive, and ultimately have a more productive meeting.

When interviewing, your goal is to learn as much as you can about the program and the faculty including teaching styles, expectations of students, retention policies, graduation rates, class size, and anything else that is important to you. Another essential aspect of a successful interview is understanding what the other person is asking and being able to articulate a response that answers that specific question.

Next, I will highlight a few of the common questions asked during graduate school and physical therapy school interviews and how to answer those questions.

1. Tell us about yourself?

This is what I call the ultimate icebreaker question. This is one of the most frequent questions asked during interviews in both academic and professional settings. This question allows the interviewer to get to know you and allows you to become comfortable talking to the interviewer. Since this is an open-ended question, it is easy to become sidetracked and ramble about irrelevant information. You want to structure your answer. Remember to talk about information relating to entering physical therapy school and becoming a physical therapist. One example would be to break the answer into three distinct parts such as how you became interested in physical therapy school, aspects of your personality that will make you a good physical therapist, and what you plan to do after you graduate from physical therapy school.

2. Why did you choose physical therapy as a career?

The purpose of this question is to learn what motivates you and what you are passionate about. As we previously discussed, everyone who wants to become a physical therapist wants to help people. But who do you want to help? Why do you want to help them? When answering this question, you want to get to the real reasons you chose physical therapy as a career.

3. Why did you apply to our program?

Many motivating factors influence why you choose a particular university. Maybe there's a familial connection, your mom or dad graduated from that same university. Maybe the location is more convenient for you or maybe you like the fact that they achieve high graduation rates. Whatever the reason may be that you choose a particular physical therapy program, this is your opportunity to demonstrate how much you know about the program to which you're applying. However, if you choose to highlight specifics about the program, mention aspects of the program that you have researched and knowledgeable about.

4. Have you ever had a time in your life when you had to face adversity? How did you handle it?

The purpose of this question is to assess how you deal with obstacles. The physical therapy curriculum is very rigorous and navigating a stressful academic program will have its' challenges. In addition to physical therapy school, you still have day-to-day life challenges to deal with. Life does not stop because you are in physical therapy school. You will need to be able to navigate any difficulties that you may face both personally and academically. When answering this question, you want to show that you can manage stress and overcome difficult situations when necessary.

5. Do you have any volunteer clinical experience? If so, what type of experience do you have?

This question will allow you to show that you were paying attention, asking questions, and taking notes while shadowing. Focus on the things that interested you the most. What have you learned from your experience? Also, you may include non-clinical volunteer experience or community service work as part of your answer. If you choose to include other non-clinical volunteer work, explain how what you learned can be used in a clinical setting to help you be a better therapist or how it can help you provide a high-quality patient experience.

6. Where do you see yourself in five years?

Physical therapy school is a three-year program. Hopefully in five years, you will be two years into your new career. Where do you want to work? Do you see yourself taking a leadership position? Do you see yourself completing a residency? Do you want to open your own practice? With this question, try to think about your short-term and long-term goals.

7. Tell us about current legislative policies affecting physical therapy? How do you feel about these policies?

I had a question similar to this during my physical therapy school interview. The purpose of this question is to assess how much you know and understand about the profession. Changes to state and federal laws and changes made by the Center for Medicaid and Medicare Services (CMS) can have a significant effect on the profession. These changes can impact the public's access to physical therapy services, how you are paid, and how much you are paid for your services. State legislative changes can be found on your state's physical therapy board/ regulatory agency website and national/federal changes can be found on the APTA website. Taking the time to research different legislative changes on the national and state levels can be extremely helpful in helping you learn more about the profession and how governmental legislation affects healthcare.

8. Tell us about a stressful situation you experienced as an undergraduate student and how did you handle it?

There are never enough questions about how you manage stress. While this question is similar to question number four above, it is more specific to your undergraduate experience. This can be an academic experience or an experience socially dealing with your peers, teachers, or administrators on campus. It can also be related to your participation and sports, student government, or other organizations while in undergrad.

9. Why do you think you would be a good physical therapist?

The purpose of this question is to determine if you understand the different aspects of patient care and delivery and if you have conducted a self-analysis to determine if your personality traits are consistent with success in this profession. This is another question that will require some self-reflection of your personality traits and attributes that would make you a good healthcare care professional and specifically a good physical therapist.

10.Why should we choose you for a spot in our physical therapy program?

This question tends to make people nervous because most people do not want to sound too arrogant when answering this question. However, it is okay to be confident and this is the time to display confidence in your capabilities to be successful in the physical therapy program. Focus on attributes that will make you a good therapist, your plans for your career as a physical therapist, how you can help impact the profession, and how you can help the community.

Chapter 7

SET YOURSELF APART

To set yourself apart, you will need to show the physical therapy program's admissions staff that you have both mental intelligence (I.Q) and emotional intelligence (E.Q). Physical therapists are constantly interacting with patients, family members, colleagues, healthcare administrators, policy makers, and other medical professionals. The work requires you to interact with people of various ethnic backgrounds, socio-economic classes, and political viewpoints. Physical therapists are continuously thinking critically, analyzing data, and solving problems, which requires them to have a high level of intellectual intelligence as well as a high level of emotional intelligence.

You want to stand out from the crowd by showing the admissions staff that you are not a one-dimensional person. Who are you outside of the classroom? What are you passionate about? How do you manage stressful situations? Are you a well-rounded person? Are you sociable? Do you like people?

Demonstrate that you are a well-rounded applicant by highlighting extracurricular and community service activities, using positive non-verbal communication, and showing personality characteristics common among physical therapists. This will help show that you are more than just another person who can study hard, retain information, and score well on an exam.

Highlight Extracurricular Activities/ Community Service/Adversity

The extracurricular activities you have taken part in (such as sports, student government, community service, etc.) should be included, along with what you have learned about yourself from those activities, how those activities have impacted you, and how those experiences can help you become a good physical therapist.

If you are passionate about advocating for the disadvantaged and underserved population, try to express to the admissions staff about how this skillset can transfer to your ability to be an advocate for your patients as a physical therapist.

If you have overcome obstacles or withstood stressful situations in your life, tell your story. Include how these experiences have positively impacted your ability to communicate, think critically, or solve problems.

Use Body Language To Your Advantage

To be a great healthcare professional, you will need excellent communication skills. While the answers you provide are important, what you do not say during your interview may be just as important.

Communication, according to psychologist Dr. Albert Mehrabian, is 7% words (verbal), 38% tonality of your voice, and 55% non-verbal (body language). This is known as the 7-38-55 rule. This means when preparing for the interview, you need to practice both verbal and non-verbal communication skills. Four important areas to focus on are gestures, vocal tone, body positioning (posture), and facial expressions. To be more memorable than other candidates, improving your ability to communicate non-verbally is a vital skill.

Gestures:

Gestures include movements of the hands, head, and any other parts of the body to help express ideas, tell your story, or help engage your listener. But be careful not to overuse them as they can become a distraction and take attention away from what you are saying.

Vocal Tone:

Vocal tone refers to the sound of your voice when you are speaking. This includes your pitch, volume, tone, and enunciation. Your vocal tone can convey confidence, fear, anger, or even nervousness. Try to speak clearly, purposefully, and with conviction that you know what you are talking about.

Body Positioning (Posture):

Your body posture can show interest or noninterest, trust or distrust. Positions that are consistent with confidence include sitting upright with your chin up and shoulders down. Slouching is not acceptable if you want to stand out in a positive way.

Facial Expressions:

The movement of your eyes and mouth while communicating can also convey competence and confidence. Try to make consistent and regular eye contact, not staring. It's natural to look away periodically when conversing. Avoid frowning.

DEMONSTRATE PERSONALITY TRAITS NEEDED FOR PHYSICAL THERAPISTS

All groups of people who are part of the same sport, profession, or hobby have similar personality characteristics. This is no different for physical therapists. Many universities and career advisors have studied and documented the personality traits of physical therapists. Here are some of the most common personality traits shared among physical therapists.

Knowledgeable

As a physical therapist, you will need to be committed to lifelong learning. Physical therapists must be able to apply evidence-based treatment methods to help patients with a variety of conditions. They must read peer reviewed journals and research to stay current with changing treatment techniques and protocols in rehabilitation. They also must complete continuing education activities and courses to remain licensed.

Compassionate

Physical therapists should care about the patients they treat. They work with patients who have disabling injuries, diseases, and conditions. The level of functional mobility lost by patients may vary from being unable to pick up a bag of groceries, to being unable to participate in a sport or unable to perform job duties. They will need a therapist who is empathetic and invested in helping them regain function and return to their normal lives. If you do not enjoy working with and around people, physical therapy may not be your best career choice.

Patient

In the real world, prognoses and recovery timelines may differ from those described in textbooks. A patient's progress or lack of progress with treatment will depend on a variety of factors including physical, cultural, emotional, and psychological. Physical therapists must be patient, remain focused, composed, and provide positive reinforcement when dealing with difficult cases.

Determined

The job of a physical therapist can sometimes be mentally demanding. Physical therapists must display a certain amount of resolve in their ability to help patients who have become frustrated and unmotivated due to a long or challenging process of rehabilitation. They must be confident and determined that they can help while providing their patients with realistic goals and expectations.

Resilient

Insurance denials for treatment, frustrated patients and families, and slow treatment progression can lead to a discouraging work environment. Physical therapists must be able to adapt and respond positively when they are in an adverse environment.

Sociable

When working in healthcare, sometimes conversations can veer outside of the typical medical topics. A physical therapist must be able to effectively communicate and engage with people of various ethnic backgrounds, socio-economic classes, and political viewpoints.

Collaborative

Physical therapists must be able to work in a team environment with other therapists, doctors, nurses, and other healthcare professionals. The ability to care for patients requires each team member to be accountable and effectively communicate throughout the process.

Try to demonstrate that you exemplify a few of these common traits when writing your essays and interviewing during the application process. A personality assessment can be helpful to learn which career type is the best for your personality type. You can learn more about your personality type by taking a personality test. Some popular personality tests are the Myers-Briggs Type Indicator, DISC Personality Test, 16 Personality Factor Questionnaire, and the SHL Occupational Personality Questionnaire.

Chapter 8

CHOOSE THE RIGHT PHYSICAL THERAPY SCHOOL

There are so many physical therapy programs available, both public and private, that choosing the right program can be intimidating. Some factors that may influence your decision include cost, location, and family. Ultimately, the decision is a personal choice. Here are tips to help you prioritize and decide which program is the right fit for you.

Why Rankings May Not Matter

Before I provide you with tips on choosing the right program, let's discuss how physical therapy schools are ranked. It's important to know that neither the American Physical Therapy Association (APTA) nor the Commission on Accreditation in Physical Therapy Education (CAPTE) ranks physical therapy programs. The most commonly used rankings for physical therapy schools are based on subjective surveys. US News and World Reports explains in its' methodology for ranking the best health schools that the "rankings are based solely on the results of peer assessment surveys sent to deans, other administrators or faculty at accredited degree programs or schools in each discipline." This means that factors such as graduation rates, retention rates, and board licensure exam pass rates are not individually measured and factored into the rankings. Also, not all programs are surveyed.

What Matters

Accreditation

Remember, CAPTE is the only accrediting agency nationally recognized by the US Department of Education and the Council for Higher Education Accreditation. If you graduate from a program that is not CAPTE accredited, you cannot take the NPTE. If you cannot take the NPTE, you cannot become a licensed physical therapist. Why waste your time and money going to a program that will not allow you to reach your goal of becoming a licensed physical therapist?

Cost

Unless you or your family are very wealthy, the cost of physical therapy school will be a factor. According to CAPTE, the annual cost of physical therapy school for public in-state programs for the 2019-2020 academic year was $66,074. The cost of public out-of-state and private programs was $112,421 and $113,497 respectively.

As of 2020 the balance of outstanding student loan debt in the United States (US) was more than 1.6 trillion dollars with physical therapists graduating with an average of $142,489 with education-related debt. If you think that's not a lot of money to owe and it will not have a significant impact on your daily life, consider this. Based on the US Department of Education data, physical therapists take an average of 16.2 years to pay off their student loans. This can influence where you decide to work, which setting you decide to practice, where you decide to live, your ability to purchase a home, your ability to take vacations and travel, your decision to get married or have children, and the amount of discretionary income you have. If this scares you and you are second guessing becoming a physical therapist, remember, this is not a phenomenon that's only related to physical therapy. Student loan debt will likely affect you no matter which profession you choose. Also keep in mind that costs include not only tuition and housing (board), but also transportation, food, books, uniforms/lab coats, etc. The goal for you is to be aware of the costs related to the program and to make an informed decision.

Location

Do you want to stay close to your family? Do you want to live in a state that you always wanted to visit? Do you want to be closer to a spouse/significant other? Do you prefer busy cities or small towns? Do you prefer warm summers or snowy winters? These are just a few questions that may influence where you choose to go to physical therapy school. Don't forget to consider the cost of the program and the cost of living in the city.

Graduation Rates/Retention Rates

One of the most important steps of becoming a physical therapist outside of getting accepted into physical therapy school is graduating from physical therapy school. The good news is that according to CAPTE the average graduation rate for accredited US programs is 96.47%. If you attend a CAPTE accredited program, you have a good chance of graduating. To get the graduation rates for specific programs you can view the school's website or contact the program directly.

NPTE Board Exam Pass Rate

A physical therapy program that best prepares you to pass the national board licensure exam is probably the most important aspect of deciding which one is the right fit for you. As with graduation rates, CAPTE accredited programs do an excellent job of preparing students to pass the NPTE. According to NPTE data, the national pass rates for first-time applicants on the licensure exam is 93% while the overall pass rate is 99%. Data for specific programs can be found on the program's website or by contacting the program directly.

Employment Rates After Graduation

As you would expect, programs with a high licensure exam pass rates will also have a higher percentage of graduates who are able to find a job after graduation. Over ninety-nine percent of graduates were able to find a job twelve months after graduation, according to CAPTE data (CAPTE, 2020). This data may also be available on the program's website. You may also ask for this information when visiting the school or when speaking with the program's representatives.

Chapter 9

SURVIVING PHYSICAL THERAPY SCHOOL

Congratulations, you have been admitted to physical therapy school. For the next three to four years, you will face one of the most challenging academic curriculums that you have ever had to endure. Gone are the days of last-minute cramming the night before an exam. Gone are the days of memorizing information just to pass the test without fully comprehending the material.

The key to surviving physical therapy school is learning how to study. You will need to learn how to think critically and fully comprehend information for the application of the concepts. Physical therapy school will require dedication and sacrifice. It will require your dedication to engage in and learn about the history, theories, techniques, and procedures of the profession you have chosen. It will require you to search and analyze research to find the best evidence-based practice methods for a certain diagnosis. It will require you to sacrifice your time. This will sometimes mean time away from your social life, friends, and family. However, it will still be important for you to keep a level of balance between your studies and personal life to maintain positive physical, mental, and emotional health.

Change Your Study Habits

There will be challenges adjusting to the physical therapy school curriculum.

For some, adjusting will be easier and for others it will be more difficult. Be open-minded, willing to adapt, and have a desire to learn when you enter the program. Even if you graduated summa cum laude or magna cum laude from your undergraduate institution, it does not guarantee that you'll do the same in physical therapy school. It is not my intention to discourage you, but rather to prepare you for success through the right mindset and focus.

If you want to change your study habits, you must first learn how to study. This requires you to understand your learning style. Are you an auditory learner or a visual learner? Are you a combination of both? Do you learn best studying alone, in groups, or both? Once you understand your learning style, it will be important to develop a study schedule.

Develop A Study Schedule

The purpose of a study schedule is to help you effectively manage your time. It will help keep you on track with all courses and assignments, help you provide adequate attention to important course material in all classes, and allow you to maintain a balance between studying and other activities. A study schedule can ultimately help reduce stress and anxiety.

Here are a few tips to help you design an effective study schedule.

●**Write it down**: Use paper or digital planner. This may include using the calendar on your smartphone, making a spreadsheet, or buying a paper academic planner.

●**Include dates and times of all courses**: If you have Pathology from 8:00 a.m. to 9:00 p.m. and Gross Anatomy lecture from 10:00 a.m. to 11:00 a.m., you will want to document and block those time periods in your planner.

●**Use your course syllabus as a guide**: Include due dates for everything in your syllabus in your planner. This should include reading deadlines, quizzes, exams, school holidays, etc.

●**Schedule study time for each course:** A commonly accepted rule in the field of education is to spend two hours studying for every one hour of class time. For example, if your fall semester is a total of twenty credit hours, plan to spend an extra 40hrs per week studying outside of class time. Another rule of thumb is to limit study blocks to one to two hours at a time for each course. You may shorten sessions to thirty to forty-five minutes if you are better with multiple brief sessions. Ultimately, you will need to figure out what works for your study style.

●**Employ your learning style:** Spend time using tools based on your learning style while studying. If you're an auditory learner, recording lectures and recording yourself asking/answering questions may be helpful. If you are a visual learner, using video, models or flash cards may be helpful.

●**Prioritize Classes/Assignments:** Prioritization will be important in maximizing your time. A common tactic is to give lower prioritization/less time to easier courses/shorter assignments and higher prioritization to harder courses/longer assignments.

●**Schedule study breaks:** Schedule study breaks to help reduce burnout and prevent fatigue. Use a timer or alarm clock to help ensure you stop and take the allotted time for your break. Remember, the study break is your time to do something you enjoy not related to what you're studying (i.e., running, painting, writing poetry, writing music, lifting weights, etc.)

●**Remove distractions:** It will be important to remove anything that can distract or interrupt you from studying. This includes turning off the television, radio, smartphone, and social media alerts. Set up a study area at home or find one or two places that you will designate as your study areas.

●**Get adequate sleep and proper hydration:** The benefits of sleep and hydration are thoroughly documented in peer reviewed research literature. The proper amount of sleep and hydration can improve concentration and mental alertness, improve your mood, support your immune system health, reduce illness, reduce weight gain, improve memory, and reduce stress. Designate time for sleep and hydration in your schedule.

●**Remain consistent:** Typically, it will take between four and six weeks to get adjusted to your study schedule. Remain consistent and adjust your schedule as necessary.

Ask For Help

It has been said that pride can be your worst enemy. However, your time in physical therapy school is not the time to make new enemies. Do not allow ego and pride to stop you from graduating. If you are struggling in a certain class or just having difficulty understanding a certain concept or treatment technique, ask one of your cohorts, your mentor, or your professor to get the additional help you need.

Study Groups

Study groups are not for everyone. If you choose to be part of a study group, it should be an actual study session focused on course content. Remember your time is valuable. You do not want to spend planned study time in a group session not covering the course material.

Don't Compete. Don't Compare

You are a competitive person. You have been admitted into the physical therapy program. You have competed against hundreds of other students and proved that you deserve a seat in the class. You have completed the competition phase. Your time in physical therapy school is an opportune time to learn to work with your cohorts. It may be difficult to "turn it off" and "take off the gloves", but some of your cohorts will become your colleagues who you may work with throughout your career. Avoid the temptation to compare grades with other classmates. Remember, your goal is to graduate and pass the national licensure exam. The only person you should be competing against is yourself.

Find A Mentor

You're probably thinking, "Why would I need a mentor, I've already been admitted to physical therapy school?" Others may think, "I'll wait until after I graduate to find a mentor."The short answer is success breeds success. A mentor who advises you throughout your physical therapy education and career can be immensely helpful. A mentor can help you navigate the challenges of a rigorous and sometimes stressful academic program as well as assist you in steering your career in the direction you want to go. When looking for a mentor, try to find a therapist whose career and accomplishments are similar to those that you would like to see for yourself.

Chapter 10

PREPARING FOR THE BOARDS

The National Physical Therapy Examination (NPTE) is developed, maintained, and updated by the Federal State Boards of Physical Therapy (FSBPT). The questions are written by physical therapists and physical therapists assistants who are trained in writing exam questions. The questions are derived from the current evidence-based research regarding physical therapy delivery of physical therapy care. Questions are reviewed by item writer coordinators and the examination development committee before being included in the examination. The exam consists of 250 questions and is divided into five sections. The testing time is five hours. Cardiopulmonary, musculoskeletal, and neuromuscular systems will make up 60% to 75% of the exam. A passing score on the exam is 600. The purpose of the NPTE is to measure if the candidate has the knowledge requirements that are expected for an entry-level physical therapist. The exam is a multiple-choice computer-based exam with one correct answer for each question. It is administered at Prometric testing centers throughout the United States (US).

Exam Content

The Physical Therapy Board Exam is composed of questions about the systems of the body and questions about the delivery of therapy. The following is a breakdown of the sections of the NPTE.

47

Systems of The Body

- Cardiovascular and Pulmonary Systems
- Musculoskeletal System
- Neuromuscular and Nervous Systems
- Integumentary System
- Metabolic and Endocrine Systems
- Gastrointestinal System
- Genitourinary System
- Lymphatic System
- System Interactions

Delivery of Physical Therapy

- Equipment, Devices, and Technologies
- Therapeutic Modalities
- Safety and Protection
- Professional Responsibilities
- Research and Evidence-Based Practice

Tips for Preparing for the Boards

Now that you've graduated from physical therapy school with your doctor of physical therapy degree, you must take and pass the NPTE to obtain your license to practice and work as a physical therapist. It does not matter how well you did in physical therapy school, there is no alternative route to obtaining your license.

Proper preparation and studying can increase your chances of passing the NPTE. The NPTE is designed to evaluate your ability to apply the knowledge you learned in physical therapy school. It assesses critical thinking skills, application of concepts, decision-making skills, and mental endurance. I was able to pass the NPTE on my first attempt. Here are a few tips to help you pass the NPTE.

1. **Develop a Study Schedule**: There are not any hard rules for a study schedule when preparing for the Boards. The most important thing is to know your study style and stick to your study schedule. Write or set reminders on your smartphone's calendar. An example of a study schedule would be 2-4 hours per day for 4-6 weeks. If you are retaking the exam, focus most of your time on areas of weakness. If you are not sure about your areas of weakness, it would be beneficial to purchase a Performance Feedback Report from the FSBPT. The cost of the report was $100 at the time of this writing.

2. **Review the NPTE Candidate Handbook**: The NPTE candidate handbook is a useful resource to help you prepare for the exam. This is a free resource that is available on the Federation of State Boards of Physical Therapy (FSBPT) website. (See appendix) The Candidate Handbook provides general information about the test, eligibility, scoring, and scheduling.

3. **Invest in a Board Study Guide**: There are several options for study guides to prepare for the NPTE. One option, The Practice Exam and Assessment Tool (PEAT) offered by the FSBPT, is a paid practice exam that consists of retired NPTE questions. The PEAT will provide you with detailed explanations about answers to the question and resources to help you understand the material. There are other study guide options that are developed by different companies. Some of these include International Educational Resources, Picmonic, McGraw Hill, Mometrix, and TherapyEd. This is not an all-inclusive list.

4. **Focus on the Big Three:** As previously stated, up to 75% of the exam will cover the cardiopulmonary, musculoskeletal, and neuromuscular systems. I cannot emphasize the importance of covering all areas when studying, but place special focus on these three areas.

5. **Take Multiple Practice Tests:** When studying for the NPTE, I took four practice exams. However, there is no magic number of practice exams you need to take. I recommend that you take as many as you can afford and complete, based on your study schedule.

6. **Don't Focus on Your Practice Exam Scores:** Remember, the practice exams are to help you find the areas in which you are weak and strengthen your knowledge in those areas, allow you to get comfortable with the format of the questions, and allow you to get comfortable sitting for a five-hour exam. If you don't score high on the practice exam, do not panic. Review the questions that were answered incorrectly and focus on improving your knowledge and comprehension in those areas.

7. **Balance (Eat, Sleep, Rest)**: While passing the NPTE may be one of the most important things in your life at this time, remember to take proper care of your mind and body throughout this process. Do not burn yourself out. If you are mentally and physically fatigued, you increase your chances of scoring poorly on the boards. Make sure that you get proper nutrition, eat regularly, get adequate amounts of sleep, and take time to rest and take breaks away from physical therapy-related material.

After the National Physical Therapist Exam (NPTE)

Now that you've taken the NPTE it will be tempting for you to discuss the exam with classmates, look-up answers to questions you think you may have answered incorrectly, compare answers with cohorts, contact your professors with questions, or compare testing experiences and study strategies. It's human nature. However, none of these things are productive. They will only cause you undue amounts of stress, worry, and anxiety. The exam is over. There's no amount of second-guessing that will change the answers you submitted.

Instead, after you complete the NPTE, take time to decompress and reset. Studying for an exam such as the NPTE takes significant mental and physical energy. While preparing for the boards, your social life was likely affected. You may have decreased your amount of time hanging out with friends and family, reduced time taking part in hobbies or stopped exercising. Now that the exam is over, take a few days to relax. Then hit the reset button and resume the activities you've neglected and re-engage with people you've neglected.

It's time to return to your normal life.

Obtaining Your Score

Now that you have decompressed, it's time to view your scores. Your scores will be available to view for free ten days after the date of your exam. You will be able to view your exam scores on your dashboard on the FSBPT.org website. If you need to view your exam score sooner than ten days, you may request an individual score report for an additional fee. At the time of this writing the fee was $90.

If you would like information regarding how you answered specific questions on your exam in addition to your score, you may request a performance feedback report for a fee. The performance feedback report will provide a detailed breakdown of the number of questions based on a section/topic and the percentage of correct answers based on each section/topic. This report is designed to inform you of your areas where you displayed competence and areas where you may need improvement. At the time of this writing the fee for this report was $100. If you do not achieve a passing score, this report can help you prepare to retake the exam. You may take the exam three times in a twelve-month period for a lifetime maximum of six total attempts.

REFERENCES

American Physical Therapy Association. (2020a, August). *Physical Therapist Centralized Application Service 2018–2019 Applicant Data Report: 2018–2019 Admissions Cycle for the 2019 Entering Class July 2020.* https://www.apta.org

American Physical Therapy Association. (2020b, December). *APTA Physical Therapy Workforce Analysis: A Report From the American Physical Therapy Association.* https://apta.org

American Physical Therapy Association. (2021). *Comparison of Course Prerequisites by Program.* Physical Therapy Centralized Application Service. https://ptcasdirectory.apta.org/5287/Comparison-of-Course-Prerequisites-by-Program

Commission on Accreditation in Physical Therapy Education. (2020, October). *Aggregate Program Data: 2019 Physical Therapist Education Programs Fact Sheets.* https://www.capteonline.org/resources

Moffat, M. (2003). The History of Physical Therapy Practice in the United States. *Journal of Physical Therapy Education, 17*(3), 15–25.

Moffat, M. (2012). A History of Physical Therapist Education Around the World. *Journal of Physical Therapy Education, 26*(1), 13–23. https://doi.org/10.1097/00001416-201210000-00005

REFERENCES

Morse, R. (2022). *Methodology: Best Health Schools Rankings Find out how US News ranks graduate health programs.* US News and World Reports. https://www.usnews.com/education/best-graduate-schools/articles/health-schools-methodology

Vogel, E. (1967, July). *The History of Physical Therapists, United States Army.* The Fourth Mary McMillan Lecture.

APPENDIX

IMPORTANT WEBSITES AND ORGANIZATIONS

Professional Organizations

The American Physical Therapy Association (APTA): www.apta.org

The American Academy of Physical Therapy (AAPT): www.aaptnet.org

National Association of Black Physical Therapists (NABPT): www.nabpt.org

Accredited Physical Therapy Programs
Commission on Accreditation in Physical Therapy Education (CAPTE): www.capteonline.org

National Licensure Exam
Federation of State Boards of Physical Therapy (FSBPT): www.fsbpt.org

Physical Therapy Board Specialization
American Board of Physical Therapy Specialties (ABPTS): https://specialization.apta.org

Physical Therapy Political Action Committee
Physical Therapy Political Action Committee of the APTA (PTPAC): https://ptpac.apta.org

Summer Programs for Students Interested in Physical Therapy and Other Health Careers

The University of Tennessee Health Science Center: Pre-Health Scholars Program: https://www.uthsc.edu/sace/hcp/psp.php

Howard University: Summer Health Professions Education Program (SHPEP): https://medicine.howard.edu/summer-health-professions-education-program

Stanford University School of Medicine: Summer Math and Science Honors (SMASH) Medical Curriculum: https://med.stanford.edu/diversity/programs/pipeline-programs-and-events/smash-medical-curriculum.html

National Student Leadership Conference on Medicine and Healthcare: https://www.nslcleaders.org/youth-leadership-programs/summer-medical-programs/

Summer Health Professions Education Program: https://www.shpep.org/

Rutgers: Pre-College Physical Therapy Summer Academy: https://rudpt43.rutgers.edu/academics/pre-college-physical-therapy-summer-academy

Duke University School of Medicine: DPT Summer Discovery Program: https://medschool.duke.edu/education/health-professions-education-programs/doctor-physical-therapy-program/diversity-equity/dpt-summer-discovery-program

University of Delaware: Health Sciences Summer Camp: https://www.udel.edu/academics/colleges/chs/prospective-students/pipeline-program/summer-camp/

University of Southern California Division of Biokinesiology and Physical

Therapy: PT/OT Summer Institute: https://pt.usc.edu/programs/usc-pt-ot-summer-institute/

Virginia Commonwealth University: Summer Academic Enrichment Program (SAEP): https://dsei.vcu.edu/paths/programs/college/summer-academic-enrichment-program-saep/

ABOUT THE AUTHOR

Dr. Brandon Gray's interest in the physical therapy profession was born from the process of rehabilitating himself through injuries sustained as a track and field and football athlete. He is a first-generation college graduate. He attended physical therapy school at the University of Tennessee Health Science Center, where he earned his Master of Physical Therapy degree in 2002 and was honored with an induction into the Imhotep Society to recognize academic accomplishments, service, and leadership. He later received his Doctor of Physical Therapy degree from Temple University in 2007. Prior to entering physical therapy school, he completed his undergraduate studies at Tennessee State University. He was admitted to physical therapy school on his first time applying and passed the board licensure exam on his first attempt.

Dr. Gray has practiced in several different settings including sports medicine, orthopedics, home health, skilled nursing, occupational medicine, and has practiced internationally. He has treated a wide variety of patients with acute, subacute, and chronic conditions from weekend warriors to professional athletes. He has served as a manager, director, and has been a clinic owner. He is a member of the American Physical Therapy Association, Texas Physical Therapy Association, and Tennessee Physical Therapy Association. He is licensed to practice physical therapy in Texas, Tennessee, and Ohio.

Conclusion

The path to becoming a physical therapist is not the same for everyone. For some, it is their first career, while for others it is their second or third. Don't compare your journey to other students as you follow the steps outlined in this book. Move at your own pace. As you progress, remember to focus on what you can directly influence and control. This process will be challenging, but it should also be fun and enlightening at the same time.

Become a Physical Therapist is a guide to help you on your journey from the beginning to end. From choosing the best major in undergrad to passing the board licensure exam after you graduate from physical therapy school. You should have a better understanding of who physical therapists are and what the steps are to become a physical therapist.

I hope this book has provided you with the essential tools you'll need to help you on your path to becoming a physical therapist. Use it as an instructional guide, use it as a reference book, and use it as a notepad. I wish you well on your journey. Welcome to the profession of physical therapy.